| DATE DUE | | | |
|---|---|---|---|
| | | | |
| | | | |
| | | | |
| | | | |
| | | | |
| | | | |
| | | | |
| | | | |
| | | | |
| | | | |
| | | | |
| | | | |
| | | | |

**F4J16833**

**531**
**HIG**

Higgins, Nadia.

Marvelous motion

Marvelous
*MOTION*

by Nadia Higgins

illustrations by Andrés Martínez Ricci

Content Consultant:
Paul Ohmann, PhD · Associate Professor of Physics · University of St. Thomas

**visit us at  www.abdopublishing.com**

Published by Magic Wagon, a division of the ABDO Publishing Group, 8000 West 78th Street, Edina, Minnesota 55439. Copyright © 2009 by Abdo Consulting Group, Inc. International copyrights reserved in all countries. All rights reserved. No part of this book may be reproduced in any form without written permission from the publisher.

Looking Glass Library™ is a trademark and logo of Magic Wagon.

Printed in the United States.

Text by Nadia Higgins
Illustrations by Andrés Martínez Ricci
Edited by Jill Sherman
Interior layout and design by Nicole Brecke
Cover design by Nicole Brecke

**Library of Congress Cataloging-in-Publication Data**

Higgins, Nadia.
  Marvelous motion / by Nadia Higgins ; illustrated by Andrés Martínez Ricci.
     p. cm. — (Science rocks!)
  ISBN 978-1-60270-278-3
  1. Motion—Juvenile literature. 2. Force and energy—Juvenile literature. 3. Gravitation—Juvenile literature. I. Martínez Ricci, Andrés. II. Title.
  QC133.5.H55 2009
  531'.11—dc22
                    2008001612

# Table of Contents

# Move It!

Turn up the music and let's dance! Jump up and down. Shake side to side.

Your body shows just how many kinds of motion there are. *Motion* is another word for *moving*.

# The Importance of Force

What puts things in motion?

*Crack!* A swinging bat sends a baseball flying. *Vroom!* An engine powers a car. Your muscles get your body going.

A swinging bat, an engine, and your muscles provide force.

Things never move by themselves. It takes force to get them moving.

The force is not always noticeable. Invisible wind pushes clouds across the sky. It makes leaves swirl under your feet.

# Gravity's Pull

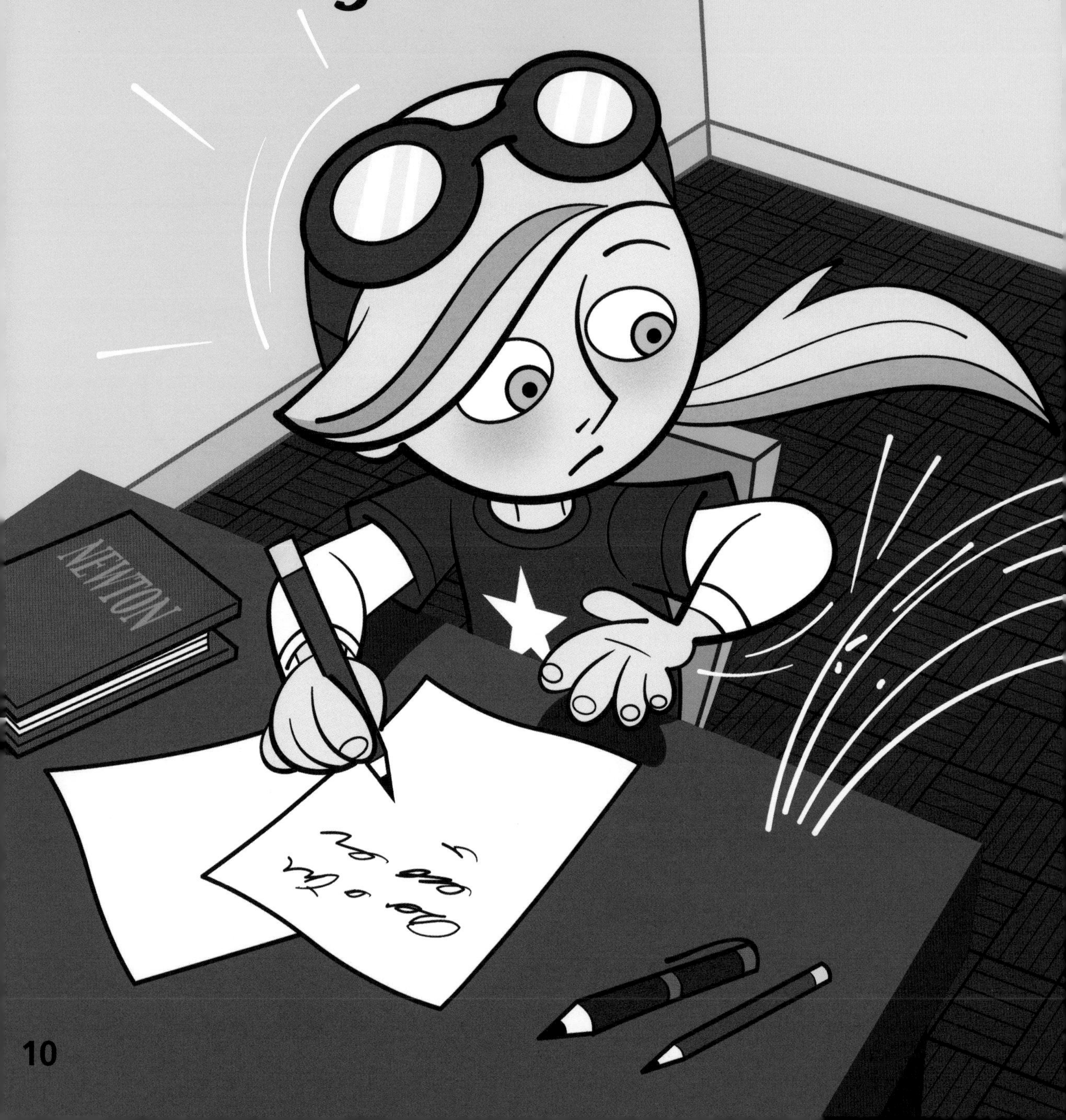

Whoops! You hit your glass and it crashed on the floor. What force pulled your glass to the ground?

Gravity is the force that pulls everything down to the ground.

Without gravity, your body would float off into outer space!

# Turning and Stopping

You are riding your bike. Watch out! A tree is in your path. What do you do? You turn your handlebars.

Things in motion do not change direction by themselves. It takes a force to make them turn.

Uh-oh. This time a fence is blocking your path.

Things in motion do not stop by themselves.
It takes a force to make them stop.

# Friction

But wait a minute! You boot a soccer ball across a field. Nobody touches it, but it still rolls to a stop. What happened?

The ball rubbed against the grass and friction was created. Friction is the force that stopped the ball.

Friction between your shoes and the ground helps you walk. Without it, you would slip and slide all over with each step.

Air rubs against moving things, too. This creates a type of friction called air resistance.

Air resistance is very powerful. It can slow down a car, a plane, or even a rocket.

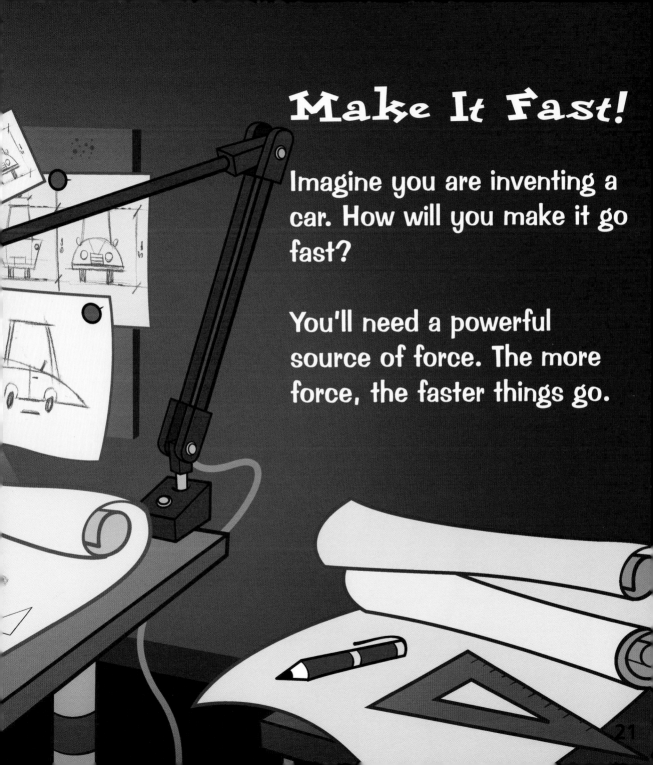

# Make It Fast!

Imagine you are inventing a car. How will you make it go fast?

You'll need a powerful source of force. The more force, the faster things go.

What will you use to make your car? Your decision will affect the car's speed.

Heavy materials will slow your car down. It takes more force to move heavy things than it does light things.

# Tricky Motion

Motion can be tricky. Think about what you do to make a scooter go forward. You push *backward* with your foot.

Let's say you're sitting on a train. The people around you do not look like they are moving.

But from outside the train, you would see that the whole train was speeding by.

Sometimes you can't even tell you're moving. Our Earth is spinning like a top. It's circling the sun. Do you feel it?

Spinning and scooting, zooming and springing, motion is all around. Isn't it marvelous?

Along the equator, Earth spins at about 1,000 miles per hour (1,600 km/h). That's about 17 times faster than a car on the highway!

# Activity

## Test Friction

Think about how much farther a soccer ball can go on the sidewalk than it can on the grass. Not all objects create the same amount of friction. What things create a lot of friction on a cookie sheet? Let's find out!

**What you need:**

A cookie sheet

A stack of books

All kinds of objects for testing friction, such as a cotton ball, a piece of ice, an eraser, a crumpled sheet of paper, and a ball. Try to use objects that are similar in shape.

**What to do:**

1. Lean the cookie sheet on the stack of books to make a ramp.

2. Put one of your objects at the top of the ramp, and watch it slide.

3. Continue with the rest of the objects.

4. Some objects slide off the ramp. Some just make it to the end, and some stop in the middle. Maybe some don't move at all. What does that tell you about how much friction these objects create?

5. Put your objects in order from those that created the most friction to least friction on the cookie sheet.

6. Examine your objects. What do the objects that created a lot of friction have in common? What do the objects that created little friction have in common?

# Fun Facts

Sound is a force that creates motion. Sound moves in waves through air like waves across a pond. As it moves, it shakes the air. Sound makes your eardrums move back and forth very quickly. This lets you hear. Have you ever heard a sound so loud that you could feel it moving in your stomach?

A rocket engine pushes fire and gas down toward Earth. This downward motion is what makes the rocket shoot up into the sky.

Air resistance keeps a skydiver alive. Air resistance against the open parachute slows the skydiver, allowing for a soft landing.

Why do you wear a seatbelt? Remember that things never stop without a force. So if your car stops short, your body will keep on moving. Something has to stop your body. A seatbelt is the force that keeps you in place.

Motion sometimes defies common sense. For 2,000 years people thought that heavy things fell faster than light things. In the 1600s, the Italian scientist Galileo proved this idea wrong. He went to the top of a tall tower and dropped two balls at the same time. One ball was heavier than the other, but they both landed at the same time.

# Glossary

**air resistance**—friction created by air.

**force**—an action that starts, changes, or stops motion; a force can be a push or a pull.

**friction**—a force created by rubbing things against each other.

**gravity**—the force that pulls objects together; gravity pulls everything on Earth downward.

**motion**—the change of position of an object.

**speed**—how fast something moves.

# On the Web

To learn more about motion, visit ABDO Publishing Company on the World Wide Web at **www.abdopublishing.com**. Web sites about motion are featured on our Book Links page. These links are routinely monitored and updated to provide the most current information available.

# Index